KOOBVILLE™

Camp Koob

Written and Illustrated by
Kristin Winovich

I hope this book fills you with as much joy as I felt creating it. Camp Koob is a wondrous adventure story, weaving in ways to enjoy reading in the wilderness.

BOOKS can teach us things we don't know. BOOKS paired with NATURE can remind us what we innately know, that is, we are each part of a larger story. Together GROWING, LEARNING AND CHANGING.

EMBRACE THE ADVENTURE
any chance you get!

Love  K.Wino

---

This is a work of fiction. Names, characters, places, and incidents are product of the author's imagination or are used fictitiously.

Copyright © 2023, Kristin Winovich

All rights reserved. No part of this book may be reproduced or used in any manner without written permission of the copyright owner except for the use of quotations in a book review. For book readings or more information, address: koobville@gmail.com.

First paperback edition: April 2023

ISBN 978-1-7334786-9-4 (paperback)

www.koobville.com

KOOBVILLE™

Camp Koob

Written and Illustrated by
Kristin Winovich

. . . until Miss Kris sounded the WAKE UP alarm.
♪♪♪ Doo Do Doo Do Doooo. ♪♪♪

Everyone gathered at the dock for roll call.

With all in attendance, Miss Kris made an announcement.

"Enjoy this beautiful day exploring Camp Koob! Tonight will be Zigs's turn to share a campfire story."

INTO THE WOODS

Zigs set off to prepare, while others found their own adventures off the hiking trail.

while Mud identified animal prints in the mud.

badger

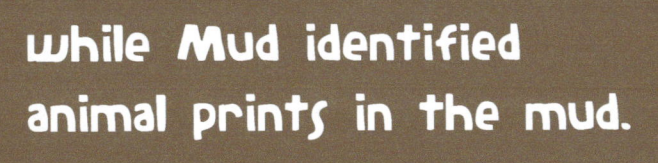

bear

wolf

crow

fox

deer

hare

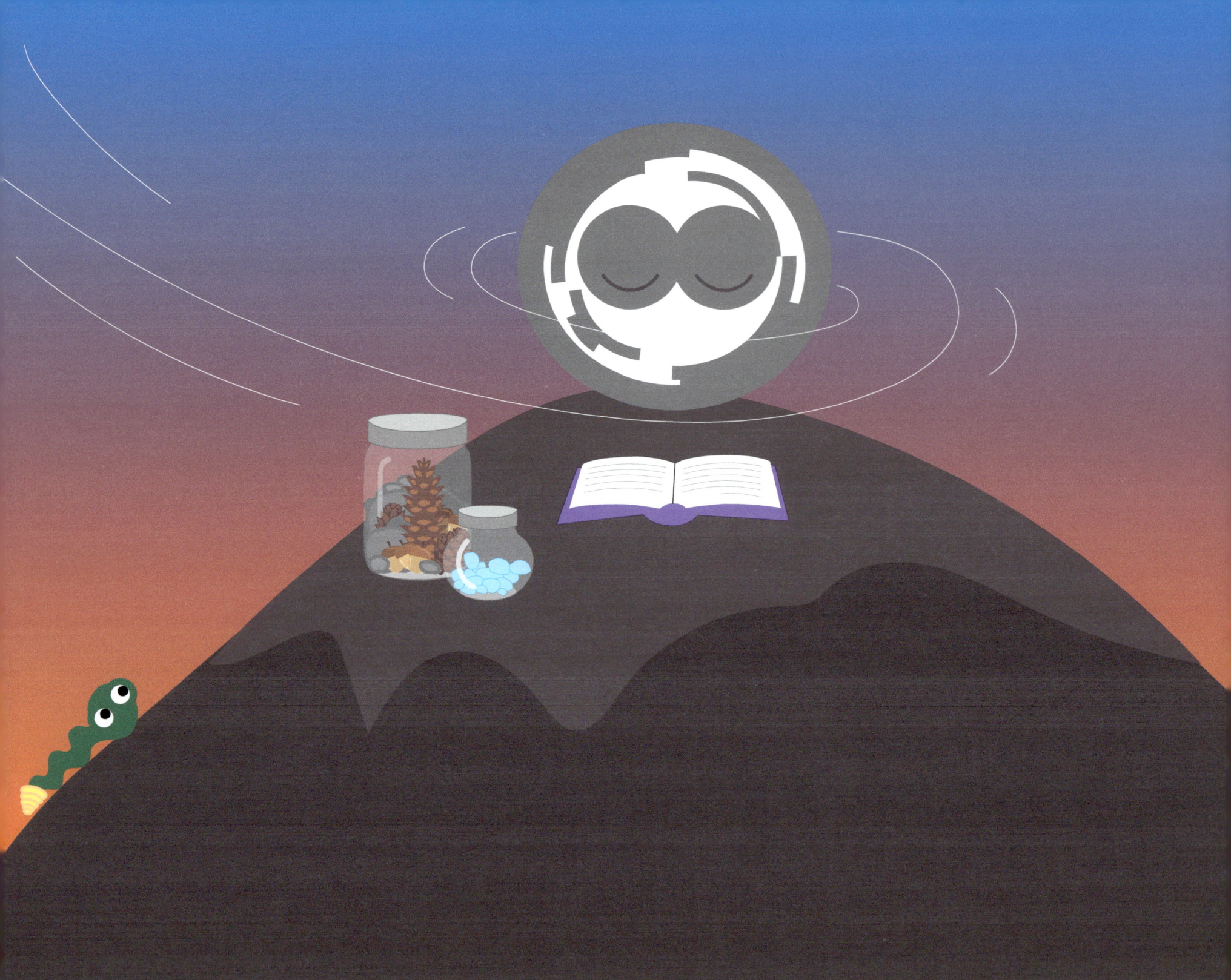

OH NO!

Zigs forgot her adventure book by a cave while hiking.

It was surely too late to find it now . . . .

How could she share a story with no book?

A BEAR WAS SLEEPING ON ZIGS'S BOOK!

What could they do? . . .

. . . Trick the bear, dressed like another bear in a sheet?

. . . Or scare the bear with a shadow then grab the book?

ZIGS THOUGHT AND THOUGHT AND THOUGHT

...until a grumbly voice came from behind.

AAAAHHHH
AAAHHHHH
AAAHHHHHH

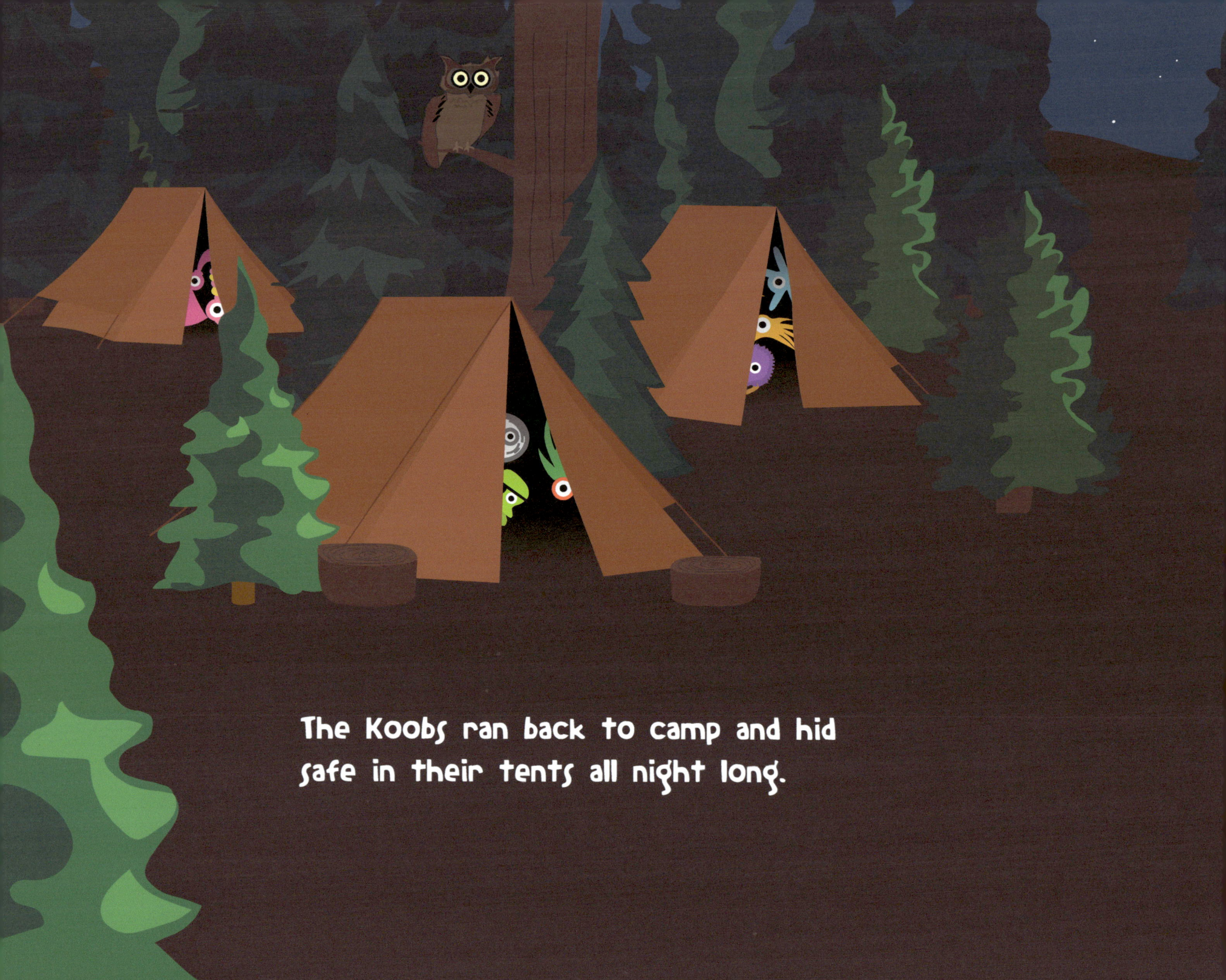

The Koobs ran back to camp and hid safe in their tents all night long.

The next morning, everyone buzzed with stories from their big bear adventure!

Zigs never got her book back, but she didn't need it....

They had made their very own adventure story to share for campfires to come!

Home in Koobville, Zigs wondered what did happen to her favorite adventure book.

. . . It was in good paws. ♥

KOOB GUIDE

GRUT

FLIRP
FLOP FLIP

MUD
ROG

WORD
NOTE

LECTRA
YAYA CLAW

GERF

WOBBLE
DUCKY

MAZER
MAZIE

BEP BEP

DOT
SHO-BO

VAMP
BOO

SQUIRM

ZIGS

BOLT
TEE

MAIL MO

PEARL

PUZZ
FUZZ GUZZ BUZZ YUZZ

QUATOE
NOTOE

SQUID
ARG

COLLECT MORE KOOBVILLE

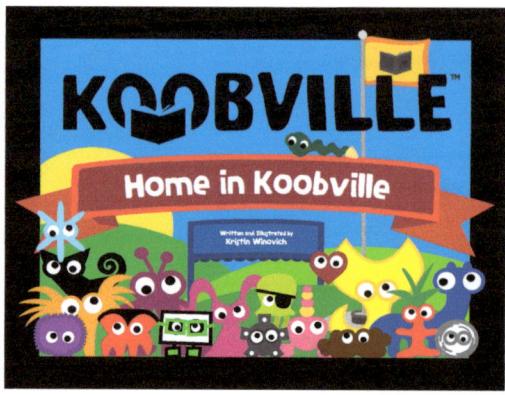

Collect more Koobville on Amazon
or support the author directly
from www.koobville.com.

Koobville loves visiting schools.
To inquire about author visits,
please email to Koobville@gmail.com.

www.ingramcontent.com/pod-product-compliance
Lightning Source LLC
Chambersburg PA
CBHW041150070526
44583CB00004B/136